The Pancake Book

Compiled by
Lorry & Gerry Hausman

Illustrated by
Bob Totten

Persea Books, Inc.

New York

Published in 1976 by

Persea Books, Inc.
P.O. Box 804
Madison Square Station
New York, N.Y. 10010

ISBN 0-89255-013-9, paper

Library of Congress Catalog No.: 76-27571
Printed in the United States of America

To Peter for the batter,
and Mike for the butter.

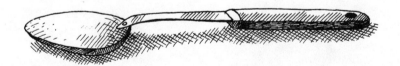

Table of Contents

INTRODUCTION

Quotation from the *Old Testament*   2

The Pancake: A Cultural Heritage   3

A Primer from the Pancake King,   10
  Or How to Cook a Pancake

Some Helpful Hints for Better Pancake Cooking   14

Basic Pancake Recipe   15

PANCAKE FAVORITES

Peter's Beer and Yogurt Pancakes   19

Gerry & Lorry's Peachy Pancakes   20

Al's Crepes   22

Al's Pan-size Fruit Pancakes   24

Patti Goldstein's Orange Butter Crepes   25

Buckwheat and Barley Pancakes   27

John's Potato Pancakes   29

Doris Hadley's Ham Apricot Crepes   31

Pauline Silverstein's Latkes   33

Pauline's Salmon or Tuna Pancakes   35

Elsbeth Cronk's Potato Pancakes   37

Pancake Fillings and Sauces   38

From Breakfast of Bears   39

Christine York's Blueberry Pancakes   40

Christine's Red Raspberry Pancakes   42

ROUND-THE-WORLD PANCAKES

Trying to Order Pancakes in New York City   46

Sprouted Wheat Berry (Pakistan) Pancakes   47

Arab Pancakes   48

Zalabee (Arab Pancakes)   49

Icelandic Pancakes   50

Hedvig's Platte Torta (Swedish Pancakes)   51

Chapattis (Indian Pancakes)   53

Scallion and Oil (Chinese) Pancakes   55

Hungarian Pancakes   58

Wilma's Palachinky (Czech Pancakes)   59

For Veron, My Borrowed Armenian Mother   61
Veron Kherdian's Armenian Pancakes   62

OLDEN DAY PANCAKES

Huckleberry Johnnycake   67
Sour Milk and Ginger Molasses Pancakes   68
Mattie's Corn Cakes   69
Rice Pancakes   71
Hoecakes   72
Flannel Cakes   73
Squash Pancakes   74
Konkapot Valley Soapstone Griddle Pancakes   75
Alpine Table Settings   78
Quote from *Hansel and Gretel*   79
Sour Milk Pancakes with Sausage and Fried Apples 80
The Pancake Man   81
New Orleans Calas, from *The National Cookbook* 82
Calas   83

FAMOUS PANCAKES OF THE WILD WEST

From *The Pimienta Pancakes*   86
George Boyer's Sourdough Pancakes   87
From *Mexican Notes*   90
Annie Sanders' Tortillas   91

Mexican Pancake Soup   93

Bannock   95

Chokecherry Wine   96

Buckwheat Pancakes   97

PANCAKES FOR THE FUN OF IT

Quote from *The Legends of Paul Bunyan*   100

Pat's Light and Lovely Shimmy Cakes   101

Pat's Sweet Sprout Pancakes   103

Garlic Parsnip Pancakes   104

Pomegranate Pancakes   105

Coconut Indian Pancakes   106

Sour Cream Pancakes   107

Date Nut Pancakes   108

Grapenut Pancakes   109

Cranapple Pancakes   110

Trish Starks' Cottage Cheese and Yogurt Pancakes   111

John's Hot Brick Pancakes   112

Soaked Bread Pancakes   113

Cattail Pollen Pancakes   114

Peanut Butter and Honey Pancakes   115

AFTERWORD

Not With a Bang But a Fizzle   118

And the people took their dough before it was leavened, their kneading troughs being bound up in their clothes upon their shoulders.

And they went forth out of the land in great haste.

And they baked unleavened cakes of the dough which they brought forth out of Egypt, for it was not leavened; because they were thrust out of Egypt, and could not tarry, neither had they prepared for themselves any victual.

Quotation from *The Old Testament.*

The Pancake: A Cultural Heritage

A pancake is defined as a thin batter cake fried in a pan. This most ancient and simplest of breads is eaten all over the world, and the role that it plays is not only as a staple food but as a cultural heritage.

In Estonia, at cabbage planting time, a big, round pancake is placed in the garden to encourage the cabbages to grow large round leaves.

In Macedonia, evil spirits abroad on New Year's Eve are burned to death by the hot pancakes sizzling in a pan.

In Britanny, pancakes and cider are set out for the dead on All Soul's Eve.

I was reared in a small town in the American Southwest. Our entertainments were simple—rodeos in the summer, ice-skating in the winter. The seasons, in a land where seasonal changes are not extreme, were marked for my family by the rituals of the Episcopal Church—Advent, Epiphany, Ash Wednesday.

It seems an anomoly to me now, the formal rituals of the Anglican Church reaching its arms out to northern New

Mexico, intoning its well-bred English phrases through the ghosts of cliff dwellers and conquistadores. Next to the corn dances of the Pueblos, or the brilliant fiestas and feast days of the Catholic saints, our celebrations always seemed isolated and ephemeral. I always felt this as a loss, as if I had been created into the central chapters of a novel without knowledge of the beginning to give me perspective, which leads to how researching pancakes has helped to place me in line with my ancestors.

One of our major social events, after Christmas and Easter, was the annual Pancake Supper. I remember this as occurring in late winter or early spring, when a heavy, wet snow might be falling. The supper was held in the Guild Hall, an old, adobe, one-room building with three-foot thick walls and fifteen-foot high ceilings. The air would be warm and steaming, heavy with the smells of freshly washed ladies and gentlemen, coffee, bacon, and Mrs. Veeder's hot pancakes, straight from her mother's old family recipe. Frail-bodied, porcelain-skinned, black-haired, and eighty, Mrs. Veeder would be calling orders in her best southern drawl, mixing a huge batch of batter, and flipping ten pancakes.

Hundreds of these golden cakes would appear on the tables and disappear in pools of sticky syrup down the throats of noisy children, gossiping old men, and proper, large-bosomed matrons. We would eat our fill and then, coincidentally, begin preparations for Ash Wednesday and Lent. If anyone were to have asked me why the Episcopalians held a Pancake Supper each year, I would have said "to make money," or "because Mrs. Veeder must like cooking them." Pancake suppers, as far as I was concerned, began and ended in the Guild Hall in Las Vegas, New Mexico.

But pancakes and the communal sharing of them have been a tradition in the Anglican Church since the fifteenth century. Shrove Tuesday, that day in late winter when our Pancake Suppers were held, is called Pancake Day throughout the British Isles. It is the day before Lent, a time of feasting and merriment, when housewives use up all the fats, eggs, and butter in their kitchens. A variety of celebrations have developed around this day.

In one part of England, school would close early, with the boys running from schoolhouse to schoolhouse, crying,

"Pancake Day,
Pancake Day,
If you don't give us a holiday,
We'll all run away."

Then they would play football through the yards and fields of the village, stopping only when exhausted, trooping home to a large and rich meal of pancakes and their trimmings.

It was also common for boys and girls of rural England to gather in the kitchen for the cooking of the pancakes after the cock's first crow on Shrove Tuesday. The youth with the greatest reputation as a late sleeper would receive the first pancake. The cakes were tossed high in the air, and there was much merrymaking if one missed the pan. In some sections of Ireland, the flour from which the pancakes were made was gathered from house to house.

There is also a game in which a pancake is tossed into a crowd. A prize goes to whomever retrieves the largest piece.

5

When England was still Catholic, the church bell would ring on the evening before Ash Wednesday to call the people to confession. To have confessed and received penance is to have been "shriven." Thus, this day became known as Shrove Tuesday. Following confession would be a supper of pancakes.

When the English became Anglican, the bell continued to be rung for services on Shrove Tuesday, and it became known as the Pancake Bell, the signal that women should start cooking pancakes for dinner.

The most famous Pancake Day celebration is held in Olney, England, where the same bell has been rung since 1445. At that time, tradition says, one woman was in the midst of cooking her pancakes when the bell rang summoning worshippers to church. Undaunted, she grabbed her hot griddle and ran, flipping pancakes as she went. (I see her flying through cobbled streets, under stone arches, scarf and apron strings sailing behind her, one hand plying hot griddle and soaring pancakes, the other holding long petticoats and skirt aloft.) This legendary woman's mad rush became an annual race, which is still held today among the women of the town.

Women who can enter the annual Pancake race must be over eighteen years of age, and must wear a hat and scarf on their heads, an apron and a skirt. The bell is rung three times; on the third ringing the women rush from their homes with their pancakes. On the way to the church, the pancakes must be turned three times—at the beginning, during the long middle stretch, and at the end before entering the church.

6

A church service follows in which the winner receives the blessing of the vicar; the vicar gets a kiss from the winner; and the bell ringers get the bedraggled pancakes.

In 1950 this pancake race became international, when the town of Liberal, Kansas, joined the English race through the aid of the transatlantic telephone. Clocks in Liberal and Olney are synchronized, and the races now held simultaneously. The race in Liberal has expanded into a three-day event in which the winner receives several prizes and the British consulate gets a kiss from the winner.

Pancakes and Shrove Tuesday have come to symbolize good luck. In Lincolnshire, England farmers throw a pancake to the barnyard rooster on this day. If the rooster eats it all himself, bad luck will come to the farm. But if he calls the hens to share the pancake, good luck is in store for the farmer and his family.

"Ill luck betides the family in which pancakes are not served up on that day."

"To eat pancakes on Shrove Tuesday and peas on Ash Wednesday will keep you in money for a year."

7

Poor Robin's Almanac in 1684 said:

> *"But hark, I hear the pancake bell*
> *And fritters make a gallant smell.*
> *The cooks are baking, frying, broiling,*
> *Stewing, mincing, cutting, boiling,*
> *Carving, gormandizing, roasting,*
> *Carbonating, cracking, slashing, toasting."*

Alice Winston

A PRIMER FROM THE PANCAKE KING,
OR HOW TO COOK A PANCAKE

Alice Brock (of Alice's Restaurant fame) once told us that she knew nothing whatever about pancakes and, in fact, could not cook them without their sticking to the pan. We thought this was a rather strange admission for a woman who could make the world's best Cock-a-Leekie Soup or Fish in Cream with Cognac. But then she said: "If you want to know anything about pancakes, ask Ray; he knows everything about them and his are the best in the world." Ray is her former husband, Ray Brock, the author of some wonderful how-to books for children, and one of the leading counterculture figures (along with Alice) of the 1960s. Ray was the one who built—or I should say, rebuilt—the church in the movie *Alice's Restaurant.*

Dear Gerry:

I have considered having "The Pancake King" engraved on my tombstone. Anyhow, to get down to cases, my recipe is very simple as far as ingredients go. Two cups of unbleached flour, a couple of tablespoons of sugar, some salt, a couple of tablespoons of baking powder, about four tablespoons of melted butter, milk or evaporated milk until soupy—usually about a cup full. I don't really measure anything, I just throw it in instinctively or from experience.

Mix all the dry stuff first with a fork or whisk, then pour in the milk, and beat. I never use a mixer or eggbeater. Then pour in the butter and beat until it is reasonably smooth and about the consistency of heavy cream. That's the easy part. The secret to good pancakes, as anything else, is in the cooking.

A good, well-seasoned, cast iron griddle is a must. The older the better. Mine is the long kind that will fit over two burners on a gas stove. The round ones are okay, too, as long as they don't have high sides—frying pans are not where it's at, as timing is of the utmost importance. The ultimate, of course, is a wood stove where the heat is uniform over the entire griddle.

Okay, get everything ready, including the people. If you're cooking sausage or bacon, have it almost cooked before you start the pancakes. The bacon, sausage, or scrapple are cooked in a separate frying pan. There is plenty of coffee perking and everything is laid out. The table is completely set, all the tools, butter, and hot syrup. The plates, ideally, are warm.

Heat the griddle over medium heat—you have to judge this by experience, but a drop of batter should bubble in a few seconds. For some reason, the first three pancakes are never very good, so just throw them to the dog and continue. A light coat of bacon grease is the best lubricant. Butter burns and sausage grease makes them stick. When the grease starts to make a round puddle at the center of the heat, ladle the batter onto it and spread it out with the bottom of the ladle. Don't touch the griddle with it because it will make them too thin there, and they'll burn.

When they start to make little bubbles and glaze over a bit, turn them, and very shortly—maybe thirty seconds—serve them. Insist that they be taken immediately, and start the next batch. Always feed the savages first, and keep cooking until everyone has had enough. Each batch has to follow the preceding without delay, as the griddle will overheat with nothing on it. Speed is important, and, of course, concentration and dedication. That's it.

Incidentally, my pancakes have been eaten on the West Coast as well as in the Virgin Islands—in the islands on a boat, you have to use about twice as much baking powder. A good variation that I tried while cooking on the *Inger*, a seventy-two-foot Baltic ketch, was the same batter with cinnamon and thin slices of apple—very good with a little nutmeg and powdered sugar.

Stay up,
Ray

HELPFUL HINTS
FOR BETTER PANCAKE COOKING

If you use fruit in your batter, let it sit for a while (½ hour) before cooking, then stir batter again. Most pancake batters will work better if you give them a "rest period" before using them.

A wooden batter-spoon works best for getting batter onto the griddle; a small mixing cup also works well. You can buy an old English batter dish for resting your spoon while cooking—keeps batter from getting everywhere.

Wheat products in your batter make excellent brown-colored pancakes; white flours and egg products will lighten the color.

Stacking pancakes in the oven will dry them out. To keep pancakes warm and fresh tasting while you are cooking, put a pot of boiling water on the stove and place a plate over it; stack pancakes on plate and cover with another plate or lid.

If using sour milk, sour cream, or any other sour dairy product, complement these with baking soda; it helps to neutralize the sourness. Also, in high altitudes use ¼ less baking soda or powder.

Most cooks say not to beat pancake batter; this is a matter of taste. Some recipes work better when beaten smooth.

Good pancakes are ½ good batter and ½ good griddle.

Pancakes can be made from almost anything in your kitchen.

BASIC PANCAKE RECIPE

1½ cups white flour
1 teaspoon salt
3 tablespoons sugar
2 teaspoons baking powder
2 eggs
1¼ cups milk
3 tablespoons vegetable oil

Mix flour, salt, sugar and the baking powder together well. Add the eggs, beaten lightly, to the milk, then pour the milk mixture into the dry ingredients and mix until moistened. Last of all, put the oil in and give it a few more stirs.

BASIC COOKING INSTRUCTIONS

Preheat your griddle or pan until it's hot enough for water to bounce off it. Pour batter on the griddle from a spoon or ladle. When little bubbles appear on the top, peek underneath, and see if the cake is brown, then turn and finish cooking. Don't turn it twice. Serve the pancakes at once with your favorite topping.

NOTE: All of the recipes in this book will serve 4 - 6 people.

Pancake Favorites

Peter Lauritzen, who happens to be one of the world's best pancake chefs and, at the same time, a very worthy cousin, is the original inspiration for this book, which began as a series of Sunday breakfasts. "Let's see how many different kinds of pancakes we can make and eat every Sunday, every week for the rest of our lives." That was our original idea, only Cousin Peter was the one who ended up doing all the cooking, and we the crazy eating.

Then, after a year of wading in syrup and wearing butter pats for hats, we decided that a Sunday pancake breakfast made a better book than a meal, because as a meal it was beginning to get tiresome. At this point, I was thinking about fairy tale kings and pancake princes and treasuries full of pancake currency. Fantasies of this sort made my cousin all the more sick, but by then I was racing around with a spatula in my hand and filling my car with maple syrup instead of gas. And it was no longer Sunday morning, it was every day of the world—a National Pancake Holiday!

And that's how this book began.

PETER'S BEER AND YOGURT PANCAKES

2 cups white unbleached flour
1/3 cup bran or whole wheat flour
1 tablespoon baking powder
1/4 teaspoon salt
2 eggs
1/4 cup honey
1 cup quality imported beer, preferably dark
8 ounces plain yogurt
1 cup milk
1/3 cup bacon or sausage drippings

Mix flour, baking powder, salt; then, while stirring vigorously, add eggs, honey, beer, yogurt, milk, and drippings. Continue to stir until most of the lumps are gone. Allow batter to rest for a few minutes "until seething stops."

Griddle preference here is for an unsoaped, unscraped, cast iron or aluminum griddle. Surface should be smooth and have a nice patina. Wipe on vegetable oil with a paper towel before griddle is placed over flame.

Flame or range should be set just below high heat. Peter allows griddle to preheat a good 5 to 10 minutes before pouring on batter with a soup ladle. When griddle is smoking hot, pancakes are ready to go on.

Peter's pancakes are large—6 to 8 inches in diameter and quite thin. You may add more or less milk to his recipe, depending on what thickness you desire.

GERRY AND LORRY'S PEACHY PANCAKES

3 eggs
1 tablespoon oil or butter
2/3 cup milk
1/3 cup syrup (from canned cling peaches)
3/4 cup white flour
1/4 teaspoon salt
1 teaspoon baking powder
1 16 ounce can cling peach slices (2 cups)
1 pound creamed cottage cheese (for filling)

Beat eggs in a bowl until well mixed; add oil, milk, peach syrup and blend. Sift dry ingredients together and add egg and milk mixture; beat until smooth. Allow batter to sit at room temperature for one hour (overnight is best). Before making pancakes, dice or thinly re-slice cling peach slices. To make pancakes, use a 6″ to 8″ crepe pan, or a well-seasoned, small frying pan; preheat at 250° for 5 minutes. Butter pan for each pancake. Ladle batter into pan and tip so that batter spreads evenly. Add peach slices and pour a small additional quantity of batter over them. Cook until edges turn brown and flip. Keep pancakes on rack in pre-heated oven.

Sauce:

1 16 ounce can cling peach slices (2 cups)
1/3 cup orange juice
1 1/2 teaspoon grated orange rind
2 tablespoons brandy (optional)

Place cling peaches in blender; add orange juice, grated orange rind, brandy. Blend well and warm. Spread creamed cottage cheese in even layers between stacked pancakes. Garnish with peach slices. Pour sauce over top and serve.

AL'S CREPES

Al Weinman is the owner and chef of a restaurant called The Restaurant in Lenox, Massachusetts. When I interviewed Al on the subject of pancakes and crepes, he had this to say: "I don't like syrup—you might as well put it on hot white bread. Pancakes are really best for fruits and savories. Crepes, unlike pancakes, can be stored for a period of up to four days; you can freeze them if you put wax paper between each one."

About crepe pan preparation:
"This is for a new or old heavy gauge aluminum pan, 9″ to 10″ wide. Put in enough salt to cover the pan at least 1/4″ thick. Place over a medium flame and move the salt around every now and then. Follow this procedure for about 2 hours, then dump the salt, put the pan in the sink, and wipe clean with a cloth soaked in clarified butter. Let cool for about 15 minutes. You can use this pan for crepes without ever greasing it. To clean, just wipe with a dry rag. If the pan gets wet somehow, you must repeat the process. Oil is not good to use for crepes because it will leave a residue of grease. Keep your pan covered during storage so it won't get dusty."

Then the recipe for *Al's Crepes:*

> 5 extra large eggs
> good-sized pinch of salt
> half-handful sugar
> all-purpose heavy white flour
> 12 ounces light beer

Mix eggs, salt, and sugar; beat with a wire whisk. Mix in flour until ingredients have the consistency of heavy cream. Add beer, and mix all together.

Pan should be hot but not smoking. Pour 1 ounce to 1 1/2 ounces of batter into the pan and swirl the pan around over the flame as close as possible. If there is any liquid left, pour it back into the batter.

When edges start to brown, loosen them with a long, thin spatula; you can actually see the underside brown from above. If the crepe breaks when you flip it, it wasn't cooked enough.

Place first side down on a warm plate. If you are storing the crepes, allow them to come to room temperature first.

AL'S PAN-SIZE FRUIT PANCAKES

Follow same basic batter ingredients as for the crepes in previous recipe, except increase the amount of flour to make a thick paste and then add the beer. The pan should be buttered with clarified butter, and flame should be hotter than for crepes.

Turn down the flame after the pancake is in the pan, and let it cook slowly.

For the fruit: add peaches, cantalope, bananas, apples, strawberries, white grapes, and even citrus fruit if it is pressed. Sprinkle these cut up pieces on the undone side of the pancake; then place the pan in the broiler at a low flame. When the pancake rises and feels solid to the touch, put it back on the low flame; bang the pan down gently. If the pancake doesn't loosen and slide free, let it cook until it does.

Serve one at a time; garnish with brown sugar and melted butter.

For Zucchini Pancakes:
Follow same recipe and procedure as above, but first wash zucchini without removing the skin; cut off the ends, slice, and add to thinly sliced sautéd onions. Flavor with salt and pepper. Use oil to keep zucchini from sticking. When zucchini and onions are done, sprinkle with a dry white wine, turn off flame, and allow to sit on a paper towel until drained.

PATTI GOLDSTEIN'S
ORANGE BUTTER CREPES

3 eggs
1 tablespoon oil
1 cup milk
3/4 cup flour
1 tablespoon sugar
1/4 teaspoon salt

Beat eggs in a small bowl until well mixed. Add oil and milk, and blend. Sift flour, sugar, and salt together and add to egg-milk mixture. Beat until smooth.

Refrigerate the batter 2 hours minimum—overnight is best!

When ready to fry:
Heat a small pan (6" to 8" frying pan or a crepe pan) over medium heat. Lightly grease the pan and add 2 tablespoons batter. Rotate pan so dough covers bottom evenly. Lightly brown, flip, leave only a short time. Remove from pan and stack. You can then refrigerate or freeze for use later.

Orange butter:
3/4 cup (softened) butter
1/2 cup brown sugar
1/3 cup Grand Marnier or Cointreau or Triple Sec or
    Orange Juice
1/4 cup finely grated orange peel

To assemble:
Butter the least attractive side of a cooled crepe with the orange butter. Fold in half and half again; now you have a triangle. Lightly orange butter each side and place on a circular oven-proof dish. Arrange in overlapping concentric circles. Use a potato peeler to make a few strips of orange peel for decoration.

When ready to serve, put in a warm oven (about 350°) and warm through for 10 to 15 minutes.

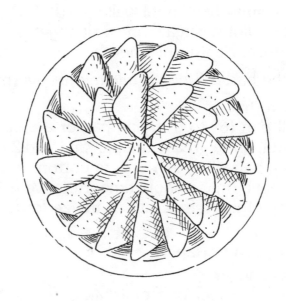

BUCKWHEAT AND BARLEY PANCAKES
(AND SOME VARIATIONS THEREOF)

When I asked a friend of mine, Noel Howard (who had just returned from a year in Switzerland studying TM) for her favorite pancake recipe, she replied that "a good recipe begins when you are thinking about the people you are cooking for; in this sense it is the people themselves that make the food. You aren't limited by what you happen to have available in your kitchen. What you have becomes what you need as you think about who you are going to cook for." This recipe was the result of Noel's thinking about certain friends of hers and what they liked to eat and what she might have for them in her kitchen.

3/4 cup buckwheat flour
1/2 cup barley flour
1 cup yogurt
water
1/4 cup sunflower seed oil
5 tablespoons sesame butter (unsalted)

Mix buckwheat flour and barley flour with a fork until smooth. In a separate bowl mix yogurt and water until it reaches the consistency of skim milk and you have a cupful. Mix the yogurt and flour, add sunflower seed oil. Stir until medium thick, add sesame butter and mix. Let sit 10 minutes. Pan or griddle should be preheated and wiped with a napkin dipped in sunflower seed oil. Cook as for regular pancake.

27

To assure that these pancakes jump off the pan with joy and into the mouths of her guests, Noel adds the following:

1. Dried apricots soaked overnight in honey and water, or, for that special person, dried pears with a bit of cinnamon for flavor and a hint of ground clove. If you use canned fruit, add the syrup to the yogurt instead of water (1/2 and 1/2). Add this after other ingredients.

2. For nutty people, add blanched slivered almonds, fried quickly in sunflower seed oil. These are sprinkled onto the pancake while it cooks.

3. Some may like bits of fried apple and cinnamon, or pineapples and banana, or grated cheese and plum jelly.

4. For a syrup, depending on which of the above variations suit your taste, try mixing some maple sugar and guava jelly with water, and simmering on the stove.

"Aquarians never measure when they cook; they trust their instincts and feelings."

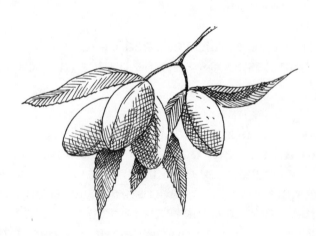

JOHN'S POTATO PANCAKES

John Pedretti owns The Toby Jug, another fine restaurant in Lenox, Massachusetts. John helped to limit my search for great pancakes. "Anything is a potential pancake," he warned, "but you have to draw the line somewhere." And then he went on to tell me how to make Hot Brick Pancakes (see page 112). After which, I happily drew the line.

On pan preparation:
"This will hold for almost any kind of cooking, but especially for pancakes and crepes. First, take an ordinary black skillet, or an omelet or crepe pan, put a good coat of oil in it and keep it over a very, very hot flame until the metal is almost ready to explode. Then take the pan over to your sink, turn it upside down, and pour cold water over the bottom. When the pan is cool, wipe it clean and use it as you normally would, but don't wash it again."

RECIPE I

2 cups raw potatoes (grated)
1 cup flour
1 cup milk
2 eggs

Mix one cup of salted raw potatoes to one cup of batter. (When grating the potatoes, use the large-holed side of the grater.) This is a southern German recipe and is best accen ted with a meat gravy.

29

RECIPE II

1 1/2 cups flour
1 1/2 cups milk
1 teaspoon baking powder
1 teaspoon salt
3 eggs, beaten
3 cups grated potatoes

Mix ingredients as you would a normal pancake. Fill pancakes with yogurt and honey, or spread them on top with applesauce. Cook until brown and crisp. Drain on absorbant napkin. Serve hot.

RECIPE III

2 tablespoons flour
2 teaspoons salt
3 eggs
3 large potatoes (chopped)

Mix flour and salt, add eggs and potatoes to a blender and blend until smooth and creamy. Cook until brown and crisp. Drain on absorbant napkin. Serve hot.

DORIS HADLEY'S HAM APRICOT CREPES

1 egg
1 cup milk
1 tablespoon melted butter or margarine
1 cup sifted flour (whole wheat or unbleached white)

1 cup apricot halves (8 ounce can)
10 thin slices boiled ham

2/3 cup sugar
1 tablespoon cornstarch
dash salt
1 1/2 cups apricot nectar (12 ounce can)
2 teaspoons lemon juice
2 tablespoons butter or margarine

Beat egg just enough to blend. Add milk, melted butter, and flour; beat smooth. Lightly grease a 6" skillet; heat. Remove from heat and add two tablespoons of batter into skillet; quickly tilt pan from side to side only. Repeat with remaining batter to make 10 crepes. Crepes may be made a day ahead and put in the refrigerator with wax paper between each crepe.

Drain apricots, reserving syrup. Place a ham slice on unbrowned side of crepe; roll up with ham slice inside. Place on a chaffing dish or skillet with apricot halves. Pour apricot sauce over all; cover and heat through. Keep warm until ready to serve.

Apricot Sauce:
Mix sugar, cornstarch, and salt. Blend the reserved apricot syrup, add nectar. Cook and stir until slightly thickened and clear. Remove from heat, add lemon juice. Stir in butter until melted.

PAULINE SILVERSTEIN'S LATKES
The Recipe of a Real Jewish Mother As Told to Her Son

"My mother has developed an intuitive quality when it comes to cooking and baking; she explains that to make something, you need a 'bissel of this, a bissel of that,' preparing it in mime with her hands in the air. This particular recipe was handed down from several generations—it is very simple, very old, and very tasty."   *David Silverstein*

> 5 pounds potatoes
> 4 eggs
> 1 tablespoon salt
> a *bissel* (pinch) pepper
> a *bissel* paprika
> matzah meal
> vegetable oil
> sour cream, honey, or yogurt

Peel, wash, and grate potatoes. Place in a large mixing bowl and remove excess water. Beat eggs in separate bowl; add salt, pepper, and paprika with enough matzah meal to make the mixture thick ("but not too thick"). Mix together until "all is nice and everything should be right."

To make Latkes, place some batter in your hands, like a kid playing with sand at the beach. Pat rhythmically and joyously in your palms until pancake emerges or molds itself into being.

Pour some oil into a preheated frying pan ("the oil should boil"). Latkes should be approximately 4" in diameter. Put as many as you can fit into the pan, and cook until brown.

"To remove excess oil, place paper towel or napkin under Latka and use same paper to blot over (saves paper)." Top with sour cream, yogurt, or honey.

PAULINE'S SALMON OR TUNA PANCAKES

Large can salmon or tuna fish
1 medium potato
1 small onion
bissel (pinch) pepper, paprika, garlic
1 cup matzah meal
2 eggs, beaten
2 ounces seltzer or club soda
2 ounces milk

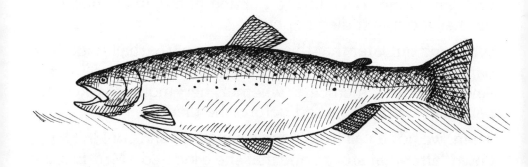

Remove juice from salmon or tuna can; place in mixing bowl and remove soft bones. Peel and grate potato and onion; add pepper, paprika, garlic. In separate bowl mix matzah meal, milk and eggs; add "one long spritz of seltzer or club soda (2 ounces)."

Caution: "Make sure you take the bones out (just in case)."

Now mix all together thoroughly.

"Put the oil on the fire with the frying pan between, and boil the oil."

Follow previous patting technique.

One day we heard a great pancake story. Our Aunt Glad, who gave us considerable help on this book, phoned to say an old friend of our family, Amy Duvall, had a recipe for French Potato Pancakes that was 500 years old. Glad said that when Amy's mother was alive and staying in a nursing home, she had asked Amy for a last request: a potato pancake cooked in the old family style. Amy cooked it and brought it right over to the nursing home, whereupon her mother ate it and died happy.

We found out later that this story was only partially true. The pancake wasn't French, it was German. Amy can't cook. And nobody remembers whether her mother asked for pancakes or potato salad before she died.

Then, we got a call from Amy saying that she couldn't let us down "after that story," and that she'd located a Mrs. Elsbeth Cronk whose potato pancakes were really worth bragging about. The following recipe may not be worth dying for, but we swear it's true.

ELSBETH CRONK'S POTATO PANCAKES

2 potatoes shredded
2 onions shredded
flour or bran flakes
1 beaten egg

The potatoes must be shredded not grated, because grating makes them too wet. Mrs. Cronk uses a Moulay grinder; the potatoes and the onions should be shredded together and the water or juice from them should be kept. Add flour or bran flakes and beaten egg to get a consistency similar to oatmeal. (It shouldn't be too stiff.) If the consistency's too stiff add some of the onion-potato water until it's right.

Cook in an electric frying pan in hot grease or oil. The pancake should be *crisp* around the edges and thin.

Serve with applesauce or stewed blueberry topping.

PANCAKE FILLINGS AND SAUCES

1. Hash made from any leftover meat simmered down with tomatoes and chopped onions.

2. Corned beef hash, spiced with evaporated milk and eggs. (Roll up in buckwheat cakes.)

3. Chili beans (corn cake).

4. Chili served with barbecue sauce.

5. Cottage cheese mashed with chives.

6. Fry pork sausages and make a brown pan gravy of the grease; roll up sausage in pancake. Pour gravy over.

7. Place thin strips of barbecue beef inside pancake with barbecue sauce, and roll up.

8. Use stewed fruit with sour cream or cottage cheese.

9. Make chicken a la king; roll up in pancake.

10. Bake pancake with cheddar cheese wedge tucked inside.

Over the alpine blueberry barrens,
bears roam, rake and glut.
We hoard buckets-full back
to camp, to hot griddles and
churning bellies...
enough for every star gazing hunger,
enough to place each star
in this sticky universal batter.

From *Breakfast of Bears*
by Aaron Schneider

CHRISTINE YORK'S BLUEBERRY PANCAKES

This recipe comes from Cooper Mills, Maine, and my friend, painter Christine York. The morning she made her fantastic pancakes, her husband, Christopher, and I jogged a half mile (his estimate) to a trout pond, jumped in, and then returned to the breakfast table, half-starved, and me a little angry because the odometer in the car going back said we had run over two miles. Apparently, Christopher's morning run was a little like stretching to him, but for me, it took a lot of Christine's blueberry pancakes to revive and restore my faith in living. I ate better than two miles worth of pancakes, and you will, too, if you try this recipe.

butter
1 1/2 cups unbleached white flour
1 teaspoon salt
3 tablespoons sugar
1 3/4 teaspoons double-acting baking powder
1 cup raw milk
2 teaspoons oil
3 beaten eggs
1 pint blueberries

Christine says: "I add wild blueberries to each cake (no mixing in the batter) and I also swear by a Revere fry pan; I know everyone says cast iron, but I've tried them all and this suits me best! Also, I always fry in butter."

"First, add butter to pan; don't let pan get too hot. Mix dry ingredients, add wet ingredients, and pour batter on pan. Place berries artistically on each cake, then add another teaspoon or so of batter; this addition of a tiny bit more batter helps puff up the cakes. Keep adding butter to pan when you start a new set of cakes, and, remember, never turn them to their original side on the pan—heavy cakes, if you do! If for some really strange reason, you don't care for blueberries, serve these cakes with powdered sugar and lemon wedges—even if you like blueberries, try this alternative. Otherwise, more butter and pure maple syrup will knock you out."

Other things that will knock you out in Maine are:

> running two miles to the local trout pond.
> the rising cost of fresh lobster.
> meeting bears on the way to the outhouse.

CHRISTINE'S RED RASPBERRY PANCAKES

"To start, pick a bunch (if possible) of red raspberries. We have our own wild bushes down the back of our land, which was cut over years ago. It is very dense and mighty hard traveling. The trick is to get the berries before the birds or the bears, usually during the season it is hotter than hell, and while picking, you're being eaten alive by mosquitoes... but when you taste these cakes, it will be worth it."

butter
3/4 cup unbleached white flour
1/2 teaspoon sea salt
3/4 teaspoons double-acting baking powder
2 tablespoons powdered sugar
2/3 cup milk
1/3 cup water
1/2 teaspoon vanilla
2 beaten eggs
raspberries

"Follow the same cooking instructions as with my Blueberry Pancakes (page 40). They can be topped with butter and powdered sugar, butter and maple syrup, butter and honey, sour cream, whipped cream. These are my very favorite pancakes. I freeze some red raspberries each year so we can devour them Christmas morning with champagne!"

Round-the-World Pancakes

TRYING TO ORDER PANCAKES IN NEW YORK CITY

Buckwheats, I sd
What? she sd
Flapjacks, I countered
What's that? she flipped back
Pannycakes, I squeaked, trying to make
everything small and easy
Huh?

Okay, two eggs over easy, black coffee

David Kherdian

SPROUTED WHEAT BERRY (PAKISTAN) PANCAKES

The Hunzas live in Pakistan in the high peaks of the Karakoram Range. Living to over 100 is not uncommon for these people, whose diet, exercise, and freedom from emotional stress have made them the subject of many "longevity probes" from the outside world.

One of the Hunzas' favorite foods (which we would not be surprised to learn contributed to their long lives) is *Deram Fiti*, a dish made from young wheat sprouts, dried and ground into flour, and cooked like crepes.

> 3/4 cup whole wheat flour
> 1/2 cup white unbleached flour
> 1 teaspoon baking powder
> 1/4 teaspoon baking soda
> 1/4 teaspoon salt
> 1 or 2 eggs
> 1 1/4 cups milk
> 1/4 cup melted butter
> 2 tablespoons honey
> 1/2 cup wheat sprouts

Mix flours; add baking powder, baking soda, and salt. Mix well. Mix separately eggs, milk, butter, and honey; beat well with a wooden spoon and pour into the dry ingredients. Stir wheat sprouts into the batter until they are evenly distributed.

Wheat Berry Pancakes are, quite predictably, wheaty flavored and chewy. The color is a darker brown than other pancakes. Our recommendation for size is 4" in diameter.

ARAB PANCAKES

As a matter
of fact
I don't
know nothin'
about no Arab Pancakes—
in fact,
I never thought of them
until you asked
last month—
but I
wish
I did,
because the more
I think about them
the better they taste.

Sam Hamod

ZALABEE (ARAB PANCAKES)

1/2 cup milk
1/2 cup water
1/2 pack moist yeast
2 cups unbleached white flour
dash salt
corn oil

Warm the milk and water together on a low burner; allow yeast to dissolve in same pan. Pour contents into a mixing bowl and add flour and salt; mix thoroughly. After mixing, cover dough with a towel and let dough rise overnight.

In the morning, cut a piece of dough, stretch it about 4″ to 5″ long and punch three holes in it so that it looks like this:

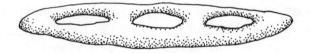

Holding it stretched, place it in hot corn oil so that it fries quickly and crisply—in the process it rises.

When lightly browned, pull out of the frying pan. Serve with honey or jelly, cinnamon and sugar, or eat plain with eggs.

ICELANDIC PANCAKES

1 cup flour
2 eggs
1/2 cup milk
2 to 3 tablespoons melted butter
2 teaspoons vanilla

Sift the flour into a small bowl. Beat the eggs and add half the milk. Stir this mixture, plus the melted butter and the vanilla, into the flour. Add enough extra milk to make a batter that has the thickness of whipping cream. Cover the bottom of a hot, lightly buttered, 5″ or 6″ skillet with a thin layer of batter by tilting the skillet slightly. Brown lightly on both sides. When cooked, spread one teaspoon of jam and a tablespoon of whipped cream over each pancake. Fold twice and serve on a warm plate.

HEDVIG'S PLATTE TORTA
(SWEDISH PANCAKES)

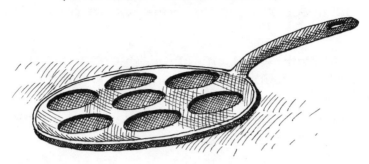

Marianne Lipsky, the fashion designer of Jenifer House in Great Barrington, Massachusetts, is a lovely blonde from southern Sweden. When we asked her for a genuine Swedish pancake recipe, she offered one that had been handed down by her family's cook, a woman by the name of Hedvig. If you want to know how Hedvig pleased the children in Marianne's family in Skane, Sweden, try these incredible dessert pancakes. They are the only ones we have ever tasted that stand up to the testimony of "melting in your mouth."

> 1 2/3 cups flour
> 1 tablespoon sugar
> 1/2 teaspoon salt
> 5 eggs
> 5 cups milk
> lingonberries (jam)
> 1/2 pint heavy cream, stiffly beaten

Sift flour, sugar, and salt. Beat eggs, add milk, and mix slowly and evenly into flour. Let stand for a couple of hours.

Use a medium hot Swedish plattar iron, well-buttered. Pour batter thinly in the wells, brown lightly, turn quickly and place on a serving platter (kept warm over a simmering pot).

Give each pancake a smear of lingonberries (for this you need a helper or four hands) and stack them close to each other. Just before serving, cover each stack with stiffly beaten heavy cream (add one tablespoon of sugar if you like it really sweet).

CHAPATTIS (INDIAN PANCAKES)

Virginia Kherdian showed us how to make this recipe. Virginia is one of those people who makes both cooking and living seem inevitable and natural, which, of course, they aren't. But in Virginia's hands, simple things become mysterious and lovely, and are invested with secret meanings. For us, these down-to-earth Indian pancakes will always suggest that the best things are right in front of us, if we'd only open our eyes and look at them.

whole wheat flour
water

Mix whole wheat flour (two cups to one cup water) into dough; knead on floured board for about 10 minutes. When the dough becomes thick and rubbery, place at room temperature in a cloth-covered bowl. For 10 or 15 minutes the dough, which has been "worked," sits in the bowl and "rests."

Sprinkle more flour on the board again. The dough should look smooth and clean, unmarked. Make walnut-sized circles of dough, then roll flat and thin and round—the size of a normal pancake.

Without oiling the preheated griddle or pan, place the chapattis on it and keep the flame high. When brown speckles appear on the bottom side, they are ready to turn. Virginia turned them with her hand. They are done when crisp.

Virginia served these pancakes rolled up with butter and honey inside. Another way is to add a little salt while they are still in the pan, and fill them with tiny cheese squares and sliced tomatoes.

Chapattis are amazingly good, and very satisfying when you're hungry. You don't have to load them inside with all kinds of goodies; the wonder of them is that they feed the soul as well as the tummy.

SCALLION AND OIL (CHINESE) PANCAKES

Cathy Bao Bean comes from an old Chinese family. She was born in Kweilin, but her family originally came from Shanghai. She left China when she was four.

I met Cathy one misty afternoon at her home near Blairstown, New Jersey. She and her husband, Bennet (he is a potter whose studio is a converted dairy barn) live in an old rambling farmhouse.

Accompanying my wife and myself were Bob and Pat Totten, who had made the discovery of Bennett's unusually sculpted pots and Cathy's Scallion and Oil Pancakes. We sat in the kitchen sipping tea while Cathy buzzed about the house caring for her toddling son, William, and talking incessantly and charmingly on a half-dozen fascinating subjects from the origin of Chinese calligraphy to Bennett's Samurai swords and snake skins, and the fact that in northern China, wheat is a staple and steamed breads, cakes and noodles are regular fare.

"Picture a melon with etchings carved all over it and hot soup inside...imagine a duck made of vegetables and mushrooms."

She went on to explain that one reason Chinese food is chopped into bite-size shape is because to cut food with a knife at the table is an offense worthy of a barbarian in the same way that it is insulting to a cook to salt food before tasting it. Even to point a teapot at someone shows a lack of tact and refinement.

In the next moment, Cathy was patting the dough into pancakes, and we had to watch carefully to get it all down. Follow this recipe and you will go on your own journey down the bamboo rivers of time.

boiling water
2 cups plain white flour
2 bunches scallions
Chinese sesame oil
salt
sesame seeds

Add enough boiling water to the flour to make a bread dough (probably about 2 cups). Let it rest for 1/2 hour, covered with a wet towel. Wash and clean the scallions; slice them very thinly with a cleaver. Use all but the very ends.

Knead your dough 2 or 3 minutes. Roll it out until it is as thin as possible without breaking. Spread on the oil liberally, sprinkle on the scallions, and then some salt over the whole thing.

Roll the dough up; you want as many layers as possible. At this stage, it can be wrapped in wax paper, put in the refrigerator, and used as needed.

Now cut your long roll into 2" lengths. Pinch end shut and roll them in sesame seeds. Then flatten them into 1/8" to 1/4" thick pancakes, about 4" in diameter. Brush a large skillet with sesame oil and let it get good and hot. Turn flame low and fry pancakes until brown on both sides. They should be the color of English muffins.

Chinese Pancakes are eaten at lunch with soup as an appetizer. Cathy says this soup can be made from leftovers, peppers, soy sauce, scallions, rice, water, ground beef, or ground pork.

HUNGARIAN PANCAKES

6 ounces flour
salt
3 tablespoons castor sugar (superfine white sugar)
2 eggs
1 pint milk
1 teaspoon beer, brandy, or wine
butter or lard

Make a smooth, rather thin batter of flour, salt, castor sugar, eggs, and milk. Add beer, brandy, or wine to make pancakes crisp and flavorful.

Preheat griddle, add lard or butter, and pour a large spoonful of batter in the middle of the pan, shaking it so the batter covers the whole surface; loosen the edges before turning.

For Hungarian Pancake Souffle:
Make same ingredients as above, except after preparing the pancakes, cut them into 1/2" strips. Mix 2 ounces grated almonds or nuts, 2 ounces raisins, and 1 ounce coarse sugar. Place this mixture into a buttered fireproof dish. Whisk the whites of 3 eggs until stiff, fold in 2 spoonfuls of castor sugar, 3 spoonfuls apricot or some other fruit jam, turn on top of the pancakes, and bake in the oven until the froth has become firm, which takes about 10 minutes in a moderate oven.

WILMA'S PALACHINKY (CZECH PANCAKES)

When we think of the quote, picked up somewhere or other—
"You can live without music and you can live without books,
but civilized man cannot live without cooks!" we immediately
recall Wilma's Palachinky.

Wilma comes from Prague, Czechoslovakia, and she is the
mother-in-law of our friend, Jan Wiener, who has taught me
everything that I know about cross-country skiing. But what
use is a downhill run when we walk like a duck from eight
servings of Palachinky?

6 heaping tablespoons flour
1/4 teaspoon salt
1 beaten egg
1 cup cold milk

Mix flour with salt, add beaten egg and milk; mix batter
thoroughly with an eggbeater.

Palachinky, the way Wilma made it, is more a technique than
a recipe. She made it seem easier than yawning, within
seconds we were all seated at the table stuffing ourselves.
The batter should be very thin, like a crepe batter. Wilma
used a cast-iron pan about 6" in diameter; the pan was
preheated and very hot. With a goose feather, she spread a
small amount of Mazola oil until the pan was lightly coated—
she repeated this process each time she made a pancake.

59

The batter was poured into the hot pan until it covered the inside. As soon as the Palachinky began to cook, Wilma shook the pan the way omelet chefs do. No spatula was used. She continued to shimmy the pan on the stove (an electric range) until blisters formed on top of the pancake; then she quite wonderfully tossed the pancake into the air, caught it with the pan, let it cook a few seconds more, and rolled it up with a spoon or two of strawberry jam. These pancakes are also good with stuffings of yogurt or ice cream, or hot chocolate syrup or powdered sugar sprinkled on top.

Wilma's recipe may be incomplete without the atmosphere that Jan conjured up for us. He put gypsy music on the record player and danced about with a wooden spoon for a fiddle and a goose feather for a bow. He told us that in Prague gypsy fiddlers were tipped by country people, who showed everybody how much money they had by pasting a bill on the sweaty forehead of the fiddler as he bowed over the table and played.

FOR VERON, MY BORROWED
ARMENIAN MOTHER

Will you watch the hummingbird
whistle around the pomegranate tree
the cat fall off the picket fence
the yogurt billow up to heaven?
While I listen to you talk
like a little girl,
while I eat my yogurt
like a good boy.

Gerald Hausman

VERON KHERDIAN'S ARMENIAN PANCAKES

1/2 teaspoon baking soda
1/2 cup plain yogurt
1 1/2 cups sifted flour
1 heaping teaspoon baking powder
2 tablespoons sugar
1/4 teaspoon salt
2/3 cup milk
2 eggs
2 tablespoons melted margarine

Mix soda with yogurt; mix flour, baking powder, sugar, and salt together. Combine soda, yogurt and milk with dry ingredients. Whip eggs and add last, along with the margarine. Bake on heavy greased griddle.

Olden Day Pancakes

During Colonial times, any small flatbread that was baked on the fireplace hearth was called a "cake" and was usually eaten at breakfast along with a mug of cider.

Corncakes were eaten at any meal. Their ingredients varied throughout the country, but usually contained one part liquid, three parts Indian meal, and one-half part flour.

Southern flatbreads included the hoecake, which was cooked inside a fireplace on the flat end of a hoe. Ashcakes were the result of mixing cornmeal grease and water; the contents were wrapped in cabbage leaves and cooked Indian style on smoldering logs.

In the North, these cakes were known as Johnnycakes or Journey Cakes, because they could be taken on long trips and would remain fresh.

HUCKLEBERRY JOHNNYCAKE

Our Aunt Glad's mother was Nellie Jane Andrews, whose pies and other baked goods were renowned in Berkshire County; she took first place at the Great Barrington Fair in Massachusetts, every year. The following recipe is over 100 years old.

> 1/2 cup butter
> 1 cup sugar
> 2 eggs
> 1 1/2 cups Indian meal
> 1 1/2 cups flour
> 2 teaspoons baking powder
> pinch of salt
> 3/4 cup of milk
> 1 quart fresh huckleberries

Nellie's only directions were to "scald one pint milk and put to three pints Indian meal and 1/2 pint flour."

The mixture, similar to bread dough, is kneaded with the hands and made into a small (4″ to 6″ cake, which is then placed into an ungreased skillet and cooked *before* the fire. If you make Johnnycake in your oven follow the same directions, except preheat oven at 350° and cook for 1/2 hour or until done.

SOUR MILK AND GINGER MOLASSES PANCAKES

2 cups cake flour
1 teaspoon salt
1/4 teaspoon baking soda
1 teaspoon ginger
2 teaspoons baking powder
2 eggs
2 ounces melted butter
2 cups sour milk
3 ounces molasses
1/2 cup boiling water

Mix flour, salt, baking soda, ginger, baking powder; mix in eggs, butter, sour milk. The molasses is dissolved in boiling water and added last. Mix together well. Cook on a hot griddle until brown.

Ginger molasses flavoring does not taste well with maple syrup. Try honey instead.

MATTIE'S CORN CAKES

Writer Paul Metcalf and his wife, Nancy, got this recipe from Mattie Soseby, who was born and raised in the remote hills of northern Georgia, where, according to Paul, one finds "an Old World gentleness and honesty—a self- sufficiency of character, if you wish—that one would never know about from reading James Dickey's *Deliverance.*

1 tablespoon flour
1 1/4 cups white corn meal
1 1/2 cups sour raw milk or buttermilk
1 egg
1/4 teaspoon soda
salt
1/2 cup water, to make a thin mixture

"Asked about her recipe for corn cakes, Mattie says, 'Mix a little flour with the meal, put in one egg, a pinch of soda, salt, add sour raw milk to make a thin mixture.'

"Translating this into measures, under her watchful eye, became a problem. First, Mattie would cook only in a heavy iron skillet on a wood stove. Because we happen to have both, and perhaps out of love for Mattie, we still fry our cakes this way, have never tried any other. With your pan over an electric stove, they may be just as good, but we make no guarantees. Second, Mattie insisted on water-ground white corn meal from Nora Mills in Helen, Georgia. So long as we have this supply, we use it—but water-ground white corn meal is available elsewhere. Third, sour raw milk may be hard to locate, but we find that buttermilk does just as well. And last, we have made one addition—or corruption—that we think helps the consistency; we add a little water to the batter.

"Fry these cakes in drippings over a good hardwood fire, and if you happen to have a few slices of baked country ham and a fresh spinach, grapefruit, and radish salad—Lordy, you have dined!"

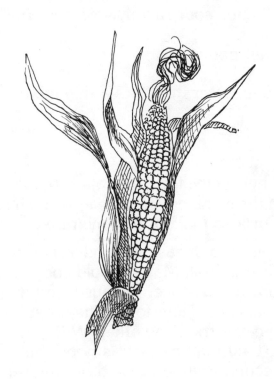

RICE PANCAKES

3 pints cold water
3/4 cup white rice
3 cups milk
1 teaspoon salt
flour

Put about three pints of cold water over the rice, stir with a silver fork and let heat to the boiling point over a quick fire. Let boil 3 or 4 minutes, pour into a sieve, and let cold water run through the rice to blanch it.

Put the blanched rice into a double boiler with about 3 cups of milk. Let cook undisturbed until the rice is tender and the milk absorbed. Add salt when about half cooked. Turn the rice on a shallow dish.

When cool enough to handle, shape into round, flat cakes 3/4" thick. Pat them in flour on each side and sauté in hot salt pork until nicely browned on both sides.

These may be served at dinner with a special treat of Honey Syrup, which is made by boiling 2 cups of granulated sugar and 1 cup of boiling water, washing down and covering the saucepan as in making fondant, about 6 minutes. Add 4 tablespoons of strained honey. Serve cold.

HOECAKES

1 cup white corn meal
1/2 teaspoon salt
1 teaspoon sugar
boiling milk or water enough to scald it

Mixture must be thick enough so it will not spread on griddle. Grease the griddle with salt pork, drop the mixture on with a large spoon. Pat the cakes out until about 1/2" thick; cook them slowly, and when browned put a bit of butter on the top of each cake and turn them over. They cannot cook too long, provided they do not burn.

Sometimes the dough is put on in one large cake, and as soon as it is brown underneath, it is turned over upon a freshly greased place; the thin, crisp crust is peeled off with a knife, laid on a hot plate, and spread with butter, and when another brown crust is formed, the cake is turned again, the crust is removed and buttered, and so on until the cake is all browned. These crisp, buttered crusts are served piled together and cut in sections.

FLANNEL CAKES

1 pint milk
1/3 cup yeast
1 pint flour
1/2 teaspoon salt
1 egg
1 tablespoon melted butter

The night before serving, mix milk, yeast, and flour. In the morning, add salt, egg (with the yolk and white beaten separately), and melted butter. You may vary this recipe by using half or one-third fine white corn meal or graham flour with the white flour.

SQUASH PANCAKES

1 cup boiling milk
1 cup strained squash
1 tablespoon butter
1 tablespoon sugar
1/2 teaspoon salt
1 egg
2 teaspoons baking powder
1 cup flour

Pour the boiling milk into the squash; add the butter, sugar, and salt. When cool, add the egg, well beaten; then the baking powder, mixed and sifted with the flour. If too thin, use more flour; if too thick, add a little more milk.

KONKAPOT VALLEY
SOAPSTONE GRIDDLE PANCAKES

Karl Lipsky, the creator and owner of New England's largest Americana gift barn—Jenifer House, in Great Barrington, Massachusetts—lives well off the beaten path. Karl's and Marianne's home inside and out is something from a painting by Grandma Moses; in every detail it reflects a time when people lived more quietly, fires burned more cheerily, and pancakes tasted as though they had just hopped off a soapstone griddle. Don't accuse us of romanticizing until you've tried Karl's griddle pancakes.

1 1/2 cups all-purpose flour
1 cup dry, unseasoned bread crumbs
3 ounces sugar
1 teaspoon salt
2 teaspoons baking powder
3 extra large eggs
2 cups milk
1 ounce corn oil
1 ounce melted butter

Mix all-purpose flour, bread crumbs, sugar, salt, baking powder. Mix rest of ingredients separately. Combine two mixtures and mix with a wooden spoon until batter is fairly smooth. These pancakes are especially good when they are light—almost light enough to float away—so you may want to add more milk than called for here.

On a soapstone griddle, the way Karl's pancakes were prepared, you don't need any grease or oil. However, soapstone does take longer to heat, and since Karl calls for a slow flame on your gas burner or lower heat on your electric range, you should give the griddle plenty of time to heat. (Karl's griddle came from the Old Soapstone Quarry in Vermont; you can order one from Seth & Jed's Country Store at Jenifer House.)

According to Karl, it is preferable to pour the batter directly onto the griddle with a squat, salt-glazed batter pitcher. The pancakes themselves are intended to be 4″ in diameter, but you can make them larger. They should look more golden than brown and they should be slightly risen—very light and flavorful. Karl says, "They should be served with maple syrup, but do not warm the syrup because it will thin out and, contrary to popular belief, will lessen the taste."

Before finishing with Karl's recipe, we'd like to add that you can use the same basic ingredients (eliminating the bread crumbs) to make Corn Pancakes or Banana Pancakes; either one will make a fine breakfast or dinner. For the Corn

Pancakes, use fresh corn if at all possible; otherwise you can substitute canned corn (1 cup). Add a few ounces of corn juice to the batter for flavoring, and remember to stir the corn kernels frequently while pouring pancakes onto the griddle, because they tend to sink to the bottom of the bowl.

Banana Pancakes are made in the same way, except we find that they work better and taste better if the bananas are not cut up or shredded and added to the batter. What we do is pour the pancakes on the griddle, and then place very thinly cut banana slices on the pancake itself. The griddle may need an extra amount of greasing for this recipe, since bananas often will stick a little to a hot surface.

ALPINE TABLE SETTINGS

When I was a little kid, my grandfather had a camp on a lake and we had cookouts on Sundays. Places were set on huge tables under the pines, and all around them were decorative settings made from pine cones, ferns, and berry branches. To this day, I can't remember a single face or a single thing we ate, but I can remember those beautiful tables and the smell of pine and fern, and sitting on stumps instead of chairs. You can easily make up your own natural table settings, but here are a few of our ideas:

Place a fern frond under each napkin.

Place sugar bowl, syrup pitcher, and other china items in and around a spruce bough.

Decorate a serving platter with a circle of pine cones.

Autumn leaves make lovely table decorations.

"Such a skinny boy!" said the old woman. "You need to eat. It won't take me long to put some fat on those bones!"

So she served Hansel and Gretel huge plates of fried apples, cornbread, sausages, and pancakes. And the more they ate, the sleepier they became, until at last they lay their heads on the table and were fast asleep.

"Ha! I've got them now," the old woman cackled. "Now they will see what happens to evil little children who nibble on my house."

SOUR MILK PANCAKES
WITH SAUSAGE AND FRIED APPLES

1 1/2 cups cake flour
1 1/2 teaspoons sugar
1 teaspoon salt
1 1/4 teaspoons baking powder
1 teaspoon baking soda
2 eggs
1 1/2 cups sour milk
2 1/2 tablespoons melted butter

Mix dry ingredients well; mix wet ingredients separately and add to dry mixture. To make sour milk in a hurry, you can add 1 1/3 tablespoons lemon juice or white vinegar to fresh milk and allow to sit for 10 minutes. You also can use buttermilk instead of sour milk. These pancakes are very light and very golden.

To make fried apples:
Core and cut two cooking apples into 1/2" slices; fry until tender in sausage grease, and sprinkle with a mixture of cinnamon and sugar.

For another treat, cut up and core apples and slice them thin enough and small enough to hang on a thread in your kitchen. A string of apple wedges will decorate a kitchen and will make a children's treat that is sweet, natural, and fun to eat. Once dried, they will last forever if kept in a mason jar.

THE PANCAKE MAN
after Mississippi John Hurt

All you ladies gather round
The good sweet Pancake Man's in town

It's the Pancake Man
It's the Pancake Man

He likes his pancakes six inches around
He sells 'em fast as a hog chews corn

It's the Pancake Man
It's the Pancake Man

You all heard what Sister Johnson said
She always takes a fat cake to bed

It's the Pancake Man
It's the Pancake Man

Don't stand close to the Pancake Man
He'll flip one right in your hand

It's the Pancake Man
It's the Pancake Man

His sweet cakes don't melt away
They just get better, so the ladies say

It's the Pancake Man
Oh, Lord it's the Pancake Man

NEW ORLEANS CALAS

"One has to be middle aged to remember the old black women of New Orleans, who, in gay bandanas and spotless white aprons, went through the early morning streets of the French Quarter, crying: 'Belle Cala! Cala Tout Chaud!' The ancient Calas women are all gone, but still in old-fashioned Creole homes careful housekeepers serve calas with the morning coffee. With the passing of the quaint figure, bowl on bandana-covered head, the calas seem to have lost some of their flavor. They are still however, worth waking up for."

From *The National Cookbook*
by Sheila Hibben

CALAS

1/2 cup raw white rice
1/2 teaspoon salt
1/2 yeast cake
1/2 cup tepid rice water
2 eggs
3 tablespoons flour
2 tablespoons sugar
1/4 teaspoon grated nutmeg
powdered sugar

Wash the rice and throw it into a saucepan of boiling water with the salt; cook 40 minutes, or until quite mushy, and then drain off the water and run the rice through a sieve. Dissolve the yeast in 1/2 cup of the tepid water in which the rice has boiled; add to the rice mush, and set aside to rise overnight in a warm place.

Beat the eggs until light and add them to the risen rice; sift in the flour, and add sugar and nutmeg. Set to rise again for 1/2 hour. Heat 2″ to 3″ deep fat in a frying pan and drop the mixture into it from a spoon, forming round cakes. Take out with a skimmer. Drain on brown paper, and sprinkle with powdered sugar.

Famous Pancakes of the Wild West

"Why, Mr. Judson," says Jackson, "You've got the wrong idea. I've called on Miss Learight a few times, but not for the purpose you imagine. My object is purely a gastronomical one."

I reached for my gun.

"Any coyote," says I, "that would boast..."

"Wait a minute," he says, "til I explain...Mr. Judson, did you ever taste the pancakes that Miss Learight makes?"

"No," I told him, "I never was advised that she made any."

"They're golden sunshine," says he, "honey-browned by the ambrosial fires of Epicurus. I'd give two years of my life to get the recipe for making them pancakes. That's what I went to see Miss Learight for, but I haven't been able to get it from her. It's an old recipe that's been in the family for seventy-five years. They hand it down from one generation to another, but they don't give it away to outsiders. If I could get that recipe so I could cook them pancakes for myself on my own ranch, I'd be a happy man."

"Are you sure," I says to him, "that it ain't the hand that mixes the pancakes that you're after?"

"Look," says Jackson, "Miss Learight is a mighty nice girl, but I can assure that my intentions go no further than the gastro..." but he seen my hand going down to my holster... "than the desire to procure a copy of the pancake recipe," he finishes.

From *The Pimienta Pancakes*
by O. Henry

GEORGE BOYER'S SOURDOUGH PANCAKES

Back in the old days, there were these old guys who went around the hills looking for gold, chattering to themselves all day long as they wiggled their whiskers and waggled their gold pans in the bright streams of the West.

They were called prospectors, but they were known amongst themselves and those who'd been upwind of them as "sourdoughs." The reason was simply that they carried sourdough bread, biscuit, and pancake starter. There were no supermarkets between claims, so they did the next best thing—the yeast about their necks was kept warm and alive and ready to use anytime they needed it. Sourdough: the beery smell of old prospectors and one of the best pancakes known to man or beast.

The following recipe was given to us by a big bearded gentleman who might have passed for a sourdough himself except that he is much too elegant. For a number of years around Berkshire County, George Boyer has been known and admired as a purveyor of fine food. The first time we met him in Stockbridge, his kitchen looked like a cross between a gourmet restaurant and the Fulton Street Fish Market; there were delicacies everywhere and next to them were big slabs of meat and fish. Nowadays, George drives around with a food truck, and that famous kitchen of his kind of moves around with him—he can get you anything edible. Naturally, when we first embarked on our pancake campaign, George was one of the first people we contacted. He replied that he had a superlative recipe for sourdough pancakes that had originally come from Mrs. Egan, the wife of the former governor of Alaska. George has embellished and perfected her recipe so handsomely that we can safely say that, for our own taste, this one is our favorite in the book.

1 package dry yeast
2 tablespoons plus 1/2 teaspoon sugar
1 cup warm water
2 cans evaporated milk
1 1/2 cups whole wheat flour
2 1/2 cups white flour
4 large eggs
4 tablespoons butter
4 teaspoons baking soda
2 teaspoons salt

Step one: (must be done no later than 6 p.m. the day before you plan to serve your pancakes).

Mix yeast, 1 cup white flour, 1/2 teaspoon sugar. Add warm water and mix well. Allow to stand in a large stainless steel mixing bowl in a warm place for three hours.

Step two:
Add evaporated milk to water to make a total of four cups. Mix separately remainder white flour and all of whole wheat flour. Add wet ingredients to dry, and mix all together very well with the previously started yeast. Leave covered overnight in a warm place (The flavor is increased by longer fermentation—a 24-hour period would make even better ingredients.)

Step three: (the following morning).
Beat eggs in a mixing bowl. Melt and save butter for later use. In another bowl, mix baking soda, salt, 2 tablespoons sugar. Place dry ingredients into beaten eggs and beat some more. Pour mixture into sourdough batter. Add melted butter and gently fold.

George used an electric griddle for his sourdoughs. He kept the temperature at 400°; the griddle was preheated for about 10 minutes and greased with a piece of ham fat. George's pancakes were spooned on 6 at a time; each pancake was about 6 inches in diameter.

As the bubbles on the surface broke and the pancake began to look less shiny and more dull in appearance, they were ready to flip. The color was a rich and dark brown.

"The Tortilla, the almost universal country substitute for bread, is a cake made of maize and about the size of a large buckwheat cake. In almost every hut and garden, one can hear the grinding and the patting of the Tortilla. Seated on the ground, the woman has beside her a dish of soaking grains of maize. In front of her is a curved stone, and upon this she mashes the maize with a stone roller held in both hands until it is a paste. The paste she moulds and skilfully pats into shape, and lays upon a piece of sheet iron to bake over a charcoal fire."

From *Mexican Notes*
by Charles Dudley Warner

ANNIE SANDERS' TORTILLAS

The night Annie Sanders made the most wonderful tortillas this side of Albuquerque in Housatonic, Massachusetts, our children were running about yelling "Soapy pillows, soapy pillows!" They got to talking like that because we said tortillas were nothing more than round, skinny sopopillas.

It is not quite as silly as it sounds. You see, sopopillas are made the same way you make tortillas, except instead of frying them in a pan, you drop them into deep fat, and instead of shaping them round, you make them square or triangular. Also, they are not fried in grease but in cooking oil. Annie told us that if you're making sopopillas, and by accident you get some flour in your oil, you should place a real silver quarter in your skillet and "that will take care of it"—but whether she meant the quarter, the oil, the sopopillas, or the flour, we don't really know!

> 4 cups white, unbleached flour
> 1 tablespoon salt
> 1 tablespoon baking powder
> 3 tablespoons ham fat or bacon grease

Place flour, salt, and baking powder, carefully hand-sifted, into a large mixing bowl. Add enough lukewarm water to make a stiff dough; add the water a little at a time so that (ideally) the bowl is completely clean afterward. Make sure there is no powdery flour on the dough, or it will burn on the outside.

The dough should be formed into rolls the size of a golf ball. Let them sit for about 20 minutes.

Next, pat the rolls with your hands, making a slapping sound—Annie says this can be done only if you have Mexican or Indian blood, but we saw her do it, and Pauline Silverstein does the same thing when she's making Latkes, so don't worry. If you can't make music with the dough in your palms, simply roll it out with a roller so that each one is 6″ to 8″ in circumference and 1/8″ to 1/4″ thick.

Place tortillas on a hot, ungreased griddle until bubbles appear; these bubbles or blisters won't pop, they will rise. Look for brown spots on the reverse side, and flip.

Tortillas are best eaten with pinto beans, which are best when purchased in a dry package rather than a can. To cook pinto beans, first soak them in water overnight. Boil them in a pot over low heat all day without salt. When adding water, always use boiling water. The real way to eat a tortilla is to use it as a scoop for pinto beans and meat. A tortilla is incredibly delicious when wrapped around a bunch of refried beans (already cooked beans mashed and fried in lard with a little garlic). Add grated cheese on top and chopped onions, some ground beef or pork, and you have a burrito.

Put cheese on a hot dog, roll a tortilla around it, and you have a tortilla dog.

Annie's recipe is very simple, but it is the distillation of years of living in New Mexico. If there is anything that she left out, it is probably this: tortillas taste best when you cook them over a wood stove chock full of piñon wood.

MEXICAN PANCAKE SOUP

1/2 cup tomato sauce
3 tablespoons oil
2 quarts well-seasoned meat broth
1 cup sifted, all-purpose flour
1 teaspoon baking powder
1/2 teaspoon salt
1 egg beaten
1 cup milk
2 chopped, hard-boiled eggs
1/2 cup butter and grated cheese
3/4 cup chopped, cooked vegetables
3/4 cup cooked chicken, pork, or beef

Place the tomato sauce and oil in a large pot; cook a few minutes, then add the meat broth. Let simmer while making pancakes.

For pancakes: sift the flour into a bowl with baking powder and salt. Mix well. Add the beaten egg and milk, and stir until smooth. Make pancakes on a hot, greased skillet; when they are brown on both sides, fill them with butter and grated cheese, vegetables, and chicken, pork, or beef.

Roll up each pancake and place two of them in each soup bowl. Pour hot soup over the pancakes until bowl is full. Sprinkle each bowl with chopped, hard-boiled egg.

"Although originally the Scottish regional name for an oatmeal griddle cake, this is a simple trail bread known to most old-time packers. It can be made in a 2-quart pan and the coals of the evening's fire, and what's left is sturdy enough to carry with you the next day for sandwiches. It's great to make on backpack trips because it's more like "real food" than anything else you're able to bring on long hauls in the mountains. Ruth and I once came out of the Wind River Mountains and were camped by a spring on Shoshone land, when a Shoshone cowboy, returning for the night, was at first so angry at seeing us there that I imagined a scene from Schneider's last stand; however, we soon mollified him with our bannock and won a friend."

Aaron Schneider

BANNOCK

3 cups flour
3 teaspoons baking powder
pinch of salt
1/2 cup dry milk
(optional: 1 fresh egg or powdered egg equivalent of one
    fresh egg or more)
1/2 stick butter or margarine

(If you're hassled, Bisquick will do as well as the first three ingredients.)

Mix all the dry ingredients together and pack them in a double plastic bag for your trip. When you're ready, just cut in the margarine, add optional egg, then mix enough water to make a stiff dough (like for drop bisquits), throw in some raisins if you like, form a ball, and place it in a greased 2-quart pot. Cover the pot and place it on a small flat rock in the center of red coals, raking the coals up the sides of the pot and checking it occasionally to see that it doesn't burn. (Ruth prefers to put the dough in greased aluminum foil rather than a pot so the whole package can be turned over in the coals. This also saves washing a pot.) The cooking time depends on the fire, but about 1/2 to 2 hours.

If you'd like to make bannock in your oven follow the same cooking instructions, except instead of the fire, preheat oven to 350° and cook for 1/2 hour or until done.

CHOKECHERRY WINE

bunchweed and bobwire
for miles

and a rig down the wind
huncht on the slope:
close your eyes,

buckwheat flapjacks
and the sunrise

From *Uintah Blue*
by Sam Hamill

96

BUCKWHEAT PANCAKES

1/2 cake yeast
1/2 cup lukewarm water
1 pint sour milk or buttermilk
2 cups buckwheat flour
2 cups sweet milk
1/4 cup white flour
1 level teaspoon cream of tartar
1/2 teaspoon salt
1 level teaspoon baking soda
1/2 teaspoon baking powder
2 level teaspoons brown sugar
1 well-beaten egg

Break up the yeast and let soak 15 minutes in lukewarm water. Add to sour milk, stir in buckwheat flour until mixture is smooth. Let work overnight. In the morning, remove and save 1 cup of batter for a starter.

Add 2 cups sweet milk, white flour, cream of tartar, salt, baking soda, baking powder, sugar, and egg. Cook, but do not grease griddle too heavily.

Pancakes for the Fun of It

"In Paul Bunyan's logging camp, the day began when the owls in the woods still thought it was night; that was when the men rolled out of the sack for breakfast, which meant pancakes cooked on a griddle bigger than two city blocks. Before the batter was poured, five big men with bacon slabs tied to their feet skated up and down and all around."

PAT'S LIGHT AND LOVELY
SHIMMY CAKES

Pat Totten, the wife of our illustrator, makes wicked pancakes! I don't know how many I've eaten at one sitting, but it must be over 20. They come off the pan yellow and light, eggy-tasting, and buttery. Speaking of eating lots of pancakes, my mother, who is 71 and weighs 97 pounds, must hold the indoor lightweight gobbler's record. At breakfast one morning, she ate 14 six-inch buckwheat pancakes, one right after the other.

If you are interested in the true world's record, here it is: Mike Veschio ate 32 (6" in diameter) pancakes with butter and syrup in 7 minutes at The Oddball Olympics (Los Angeles), May 4, 1974.

Mrs. Sally Cutter tossed a pancake 5,010 times in 65 minutes at the Island Club (Limassol, Cyprus), February 26, 1974.

        6 eggs
        4 cups milk
        2 cups flour
        1 teaspoon salt
        12 tablespoons melted butter or margarine

Break eggs into a mixing bowl, add milk, beat with a wire whisk or mixer. Add flour and salt, and mix well until smooth. (There should not be any lumps at all with this recipe.) Add butter or margarine.

101

Shimmy Cakes are cooked on an ungreased, seasoned Swedish plattar iron, which has been preheated for about 5 minutes. Ladle batter onto plattar with a batter spoon (say that fast!). Believe it or not, when pancake starts to shimmy or wiggle in the pan, it is ready to be flipped; use a fork to lift it up gently at the edges.

These cakes can be stored in an oven at about 250°. Serve them with syrup or honey, but no butter.

PAT'S SWEET SPROUT PANCAKES

4 eggs
2 cups milk or light cream
2 cups unbleached flour
2 teaspoons baking powder
2 teaspoons sugar
2 teaspoons salt
8 tablespoons melted butter or margarine
1 cup (tightly packed) wheat sprouts

Beat eggs and 2 cups milk in a mixing bowl. Mix flour, baking powder, sugar, and salt. Add to egg and milk mixture. Blend with a wooden spoon, and add melted butter; beat until smooth. If batter seems too thick add a little more milk.

Add wheat sprouts.

Griddle should be preheated with safflower oil. Pat suggests substituting 1/2 cup of finely chopped black walnuts for the wheat sprouts in the same recipe for a different flavor.

GARLIC PARSNIP PANCAKES
A fantastic winter supper recipe from Art Wood

A friend of ours in Maine, Gene Boyington of Cobblesmith Books, recently published *The Wood Cook's Cook Book* by Sarah D. Haskell. The following two unusual recipes are gratefully reprinted from that book.

> 1 1/2 cups whole wheat flour
> 3 teaspoons baking powder
> 1 egg, well-beaten
> 1/4 cup honey
> 1 3/4 cups milk
> 3 tablespoons vegetable oil
> 3 grated parsnips
> garlic to taste

Sift flour and baking powder. Mix the egg, honey, milk, and oil together; combine the two mixtures and blend well.

Saute parsnips and minced garlic cloves until soft. Add to the above mixture and cook on a hot griddle.

POMEGRANATE PANCAKES
by Leni Singerman and Eric Hopkins

1 1/2 cups warm water, warm milk, sour cream, buttermilk,
   or yogurt
1 tablespoon molasses
2 eggs
2 tablespoons vegetable oil, butter, or shortening
1 cup whole wheat flour
1/3 cup powdered milk
2 tablespoons baking powder
1/2 cup wheat germ
1 teaspoon salt
3 teaspoons brewers yeast
seeds of one pomegranate

Mix wet ingredients; mix dry ingredients and sift into wet
mixture. Add pomegranate seeds. Cook on a hot griddle and
serve with butter, honey, or syrup.

COCONUT INDIAN PANCAKES

For these pancakes, we used Erewhon Indian meal, which contains yellow corn, sunflower seeds, and chia seeds. The pancake should come out golden brown with a lovely mottled pattern. The taste is good and crunchy, and conjures up Aztec temples, banana leaves, and ancient astronauts.

1 1/2 cups all-purpose flour
1 cup Indian meal
3 ounces brown sugar
1 teaspoon salt
2 teaspoons baking powder
3 large eggs
2 cups milk
2 ounces melted butter
3 tablespoons shredded coconut

Mix flour, Indian meal, sugar, salt, baking powder; mix separately eggs, milk, butter. Pour liquid into dry ingredients and beat with a wooden spoon; stir in shredded coconut until it is well mixed.

SOUR CREAM PANCAKES

1 cup flour
1/2 teaspoon salt
1 level teaspoon baking powder
1/2 teaspoon baking soda
2 tablespoons cottage cheese
2 cups sour cream
2 egg yolks
1 teaspoon melted butter
2 egg whites, beaten stiff

Sift together flour, salt, baking powder. Stir the soda into the cottage cheese and sour cream, add the egg yolks (beaten very light) and the melted butter. Stir these into the dry ingredients and fold in egg whites. Spoon out on griddle. Do not turn the cakes more than once. Add milk to thin, if desired.

DATE NUT PANCAKES

We found this recipe in *The Ladies' Aid Society Cookbook of the First Congregational Church of Sheffield, Massachusetts.* Originally, it was Aunt Glad's recipe for Himmel Fritters.

1 1/2 cups flour
2 teaspoons baking powder
1 teaspoon salt
3 ounces sugar
3 ounces finely chopped pecans
3 ounces finely chopped dates
1 teaspoon vanilla
2 ounces peanut oil
3 eggs, well-beaten
1 1/2 cups milk
1/2 cup medium cream

Mix flour, baking powder, salt, sugar, pecans, and dates. Pecans should be chopped so that they are small enough to add crunch to the pancake; if too large, they will sink to the bottom of the batter. Dates should be treated the same. Mix separately vanilla, oil, eggs, milk, and cream. Add to dry mixture. Batter should be stirred between each round of pancakes on the griddle.

Date Nut Pancakes are wonderful as a dessert. They may be cooled slightly and served with an ice cream filler.

GRAPENUT PANCAKES

1 1/2 cups flour
2 teaspoons baking powder
1 teaspoon salt
3 ounces sugar
1/4 teaspoon baking soda
2 eggs
2 ounces melted butter
1 cup grapenuts
1 1/2 cups sour milk

Mix flour, baking powder, salt, sugar, baking soda; mix well-beaten eggs, butter separately. Add one cup grapenuts, soaked for ten minutes in sour milk, to eggs and butter, and then mix in with dry ingredients.

CRANAPPLE PANCAKES

1 1/2 cups cake flour
1 1/2 teaspoons sugar
1 teaspoon salt
1 1/4 teaspoons baking powder
1 teaspoon baking soda
2 eggs
1 1/2 cups milk
1/2 cup apple juice
2 1/2 tablespoons melted butter
1 1/2 teaspoons honey
1/2 cup cranapple sauce

Mix dry ingredients; add wet ingredients and mix well. To make cranapple sauce, mix cut apples and cranberries in water to cover; add sugar and simmer until soft.

TRISH STARK'S
COTTAGE CHEESE AND YOGURT PANCAKES

Trish Stark is co-owner of Naturally, a health food store in Denver, Colorado.

1 cup cottage cheese
1/2 cup yogurt
2 teaspoons honey
salt to taste
3/4 cup whole wheat flour
3 eggs
2 tablespoons vegetable oil
1/4 cup chopped walnuts or pecans
1/4 cup wheat germ

Mix cottage cheese to yogurt and honey, add salt and beat well with a rotary beater.

Gradually add flour, eggs, and vegetable oil to first mixture, beating well. Consistency should be lumpy. Add milk to thin, if desired. Add nuts and wheat germ, and cook on a hot, oiled grill.

JOHN'S HOT BRICK PANCAKES

John Pedretti recommends this recipe mainly for modern day prospectors, but he admits that when he was a boy growing up in Italy, he practically used to live off this pancake. It was his favorite lunch. Try it with a generous spread of real butter and eat as you would a Chapatti.

1/2 teaspoon salt
1 tablespoon water
2/3 cup flour

Make a noodle dough with salt, water, and flour. Knead for 10 minutes. Then let it stand covered, about 1 hour. Should be 1/2" to 3/8" thick. Dough should have 8" circumference.

First, make sure your fireplace has a smooth brick surface, then build a good fire over it. When the fire has burned down to ash, check the bricks by clearing them of ash to see if they are the right temperature for cooking dough; if they are red hot, let them cool down for a while.

Place dough on hot bricks and gently brush the hot ash on top of it. Make sure not to put any live coals on the dough or it will burn. Cook for 15 minutes. Dough will rise very little, but the underside will have the appearance of Vienna bread.

SOAKED BREAD PANCAKES

2 cups bread crumbs or 4 cups stale bread
  (rubbed through colander)
  milk
  1 cup flour
  1 teaspoon salt
  1 teaspoon baking soda
  1 teaspoon grated nutmeg
  2 tablespoons sugar
  2 eggs, separated

Soak bread crumbs in sufficient milk to make soft. Sift dry ingredients together, stir into well-soaked bread, add egg yolks and beat vigorously.

The batter should be thicker than for ordinary pancakes. Beat egg whites stiff and fold in just before baking. Cook well on griddle; they rise and are quite thick.

CATTAIL POLLEN PANCAKES

In late May or early June, when the cattail head is still in a thin green stalk, the staminate upper portion matures and is ready to release the golden pollen. Bend the cattail and shake the head over a clean cloth or bowl; the pollen will fall out in masses.

The following is an old Indian flat bread recipe.

> 2 cups cattail pollen
> 2 cups white flour
> 3 teaspoons baking powder
> 1 tablespoon sugar
> 2 eggs
> 1 1/2 or 2 cups milk
> 2 tablespoons melted butter

For cattail pollen pancakes substitute up to 1/2 pollen for wheat flour in a basic pancake recipe. It will give them a bright golden color and a unique flavor.

For Elderflower Pancakes:

Strip the flowerlets from elderflowers and add 1 cup or more to any basic recipe. Cook on hot griddle like any other pancake.

PEANUT BUTTER AND HONEY PANCAKES

3 ounces corn oil
1 1/2 cups evaporated milk
1/2 cup milk
3 to 4 heaping tablespoons honey
3 eggs
1 1/2 cups flour
3 teaspoons baking powder
1/4 teaspoon baking soda
5 tablespoons peanut butter
1/2 cup boiling water

Add wet ingredients to mixed dry ingredients and stir well.

Place peanut butter in boiling water; mixture should be creamy. Add to pancake batter and beat until smooth.

While cooking pancakes, stir batter bowl frequently so peanut butter stays well mixed.

These pancakes are favorites with kids. You can make them into interesting shapes and sizes because the batter is thick enough to congeal on the griddle.

Afterword

NOT WITH A BANG BUT A FIZZLE

It had been my plan to finish this book with some kind of flourish; to end it all with a pancake to beat all pancakes, a sort of John Philip Sousa Pancake, brassy and beautiful. But that wasn't the way it worked out. I got up grouchy one morning, and my wife was twice as grouchy, and our daughter was three times as grouchy, and it was a good thing we put the cats out, because they were grouchy in a way that would have been our undoing.

What kind of pancakes are you making, Lorry said.

Something loud and splashy, I said.

All you ever cook is pancakes, she said.

I can cook anything, I said, anything at all.
And it will always come out great.

Watch what you're doing, Lorry said; you're putting in too much cottage cheese and sour cream. Stop it right now, that's all the sour cream in the house!

These pancakes will be worth gold, don't worry about the sour cream.

Now what are you putting in?

Nutmeg and cinnamon and evaporated milk.

Did you put your baking soda in yet?

No, not yet.

Now what?

Applesauce, what do you think of *that?*

118

It's going to be gooey.

It's going to be the best thing you ever tasted.

It needs more flour, I can tell you that for sure.

Will you just let me cook alone?

I thought this was supposed to be *our* book?

Then why don't you help me, instead of hindering me?

Because you're so cross whenever you make pancakes.

And you? Are you always sweet and pleasant when you make them?

Hey, what are we arguing for, this is silly.

The first pancakes that hit the griddle were flops, but I expected that. I ladled some more on. They stuck to the pan like bright batches of cement. I added two tablespoons of flour, stirred it in quick, and added some diced apples, a little more milk. My ship was sinking fast. The next three were so gooey, they fizzed. Mariah came in from the living room where she had been watching Planet of the Apes and said: Those pancakes smell yucky, and I bet they taste yucky, too!

Lorry said, in a tone that sounded like Jack Benny's ghost: I told you so.

All they need is a little more oil, I said.—

What they need is the dog, Lorry said.

A futile half hour later, I called the dog in. There were some funny looking smoking things in his dish. He didn't like the look of them. He didn't like their smell either. He asked to go out. Lorry and I were through talking; our glances were like drops of water on a burning griddle. She was making bacon and eggs. I went into the bathroom to shave; the hell with it, I thought, let it all blow over. Damn that dog! The cats were back in, all three of them standing around like they were getting paid to look evil. The cats regarded the pancakes in the dog's dish as if they were so many dead gila monsters. While I was shaving, Lorry came in and gave me a hug: I'm sorry, she said. Me too, I said. You make good pancakes, she said. You do, too, I said. They *really* were yucky, I said. They really were, she said. You're always belittling, I said; you hate the way I cook. You hate the way I cook too, she said. I wonder if it would be possible to make shaving cream pancakes, I said.